SECOND WIND

PREETI BHARGAVA

FanatiXx® Publication
AM/56, Basanti Colony, Rourkela 769012, Odisha
ISO 9001:2015 Certified

By: Preeti Bhargava
ISBN: 978-93-5605-112-6
Cover Design: Sagar Chand Samal
Price: INR 300/-
Print and typeset by: BooksClub.in
Illustrations and Cover Art by **Preeti Bhargava**

Gratitude to the bitter-sweet affairs
who made me write this beauty.

Foreword

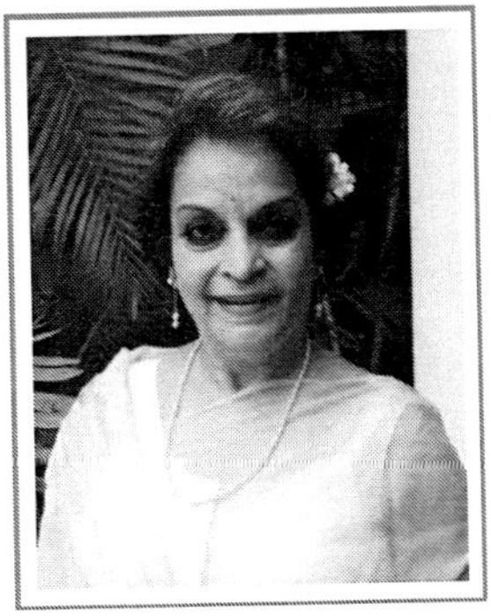

Dr. Indubala Singh

When the author Preeti Bhargava of her earlier work of 'Dear Self' looks forward to bloom this time with a touch of love of pair of eyes of a tender heart this time in her new creative avatar it seems she's floating and she is sailing steering herself up and meandering from the abysmally deep sea she was caught up into. She finds inner resilience to fly up to the soaring clouds perhaps beyond the high skies. She seems to be another version of herself now even with vulnerability embedded deep within. Yet she becomes a strong vibrant and even more than ever satiated self. In keeping with her mental state she dances away like a ballerina in tandem with a weirdness that knows no dejection and is full of felicity.

This time she brings about her own resuscitation with not a care or a doubt gnawing her about losing and she reclaims her true self. She needs no words of assurance but her inner tranquility gushes forth and she glides exquisitely with her unconditional love. Poignantly with serendipity, she strives to see no destruction of her redundant self. She finds her rhythm to pause and dance on with sure confident steps which she has evolved with her own crazy ingenuity from dawn to dusk engulfed in the ethereal nature entrapped in a snowy graceful gown. Submerged in its entirety, and the very belief that it was the cocooned cosmos of her being. She breaks through it courageously to come forth to bloom afresh truly with a mesmerizing radiant fragrance of its aura all around spreading a serenity as a balm. This is pacifying not only to her very soul but also to those who bruised her and left her fettered her unhealed bleeding wounds.

However now her rejuvenated self with a cleansed self basking in the bitter-sweet memories strides ahead refurbished.

The awe-inspiring illustrations accompanying unfolding her self gloriously seems to make her reach and to those elusive ecstatic heights of her own being. Despite being caught up in a whirlpool of emotions where she might have submerged her beautiful inner self she cajoles and endures with her inner strivings. In the process, she arises like a Phoenix to awaken to her true creative self to reclaim her very being. Rather than being bitter about her no-so-pleasant memories at times, she ruminates and reflects upon them with gratitude to find her eternal beauty within.

I couldn't think of a more befitting analogy by Elizabeth Gilbert, "The Universe buries strange jewels deep within us all and then stands back to see if we find them."

Dr. Indubala Singh
(Prof. of English retd.)

About The Author

A graduate in Fine Arts in Graphics, Preeti Bhargava always had a flair for doing something unique and creative.

'To express is to be human', is what the author of 'Dear Self', Preeti Bhargava believes in. She is a seeker, who has an ingenious mind and sees herself as a nomad while she romances with metaphors and similes.

Her poems are nothing but reflections of her true self and the artistic side of life.

Professionally, she is an artist, a wall decorator and a visual creative designer. Amidst her busy schedule, her cravings for solace are fulfilled by writing.

You can get in touch with her at
preeti@fourhands.in
Or
Scan the QR code for the Website

[bringing together words to comfort you]

i bloom when
you touch me
with your eyes,
hold me in your heart.
touch me with love
or else
touch me not.

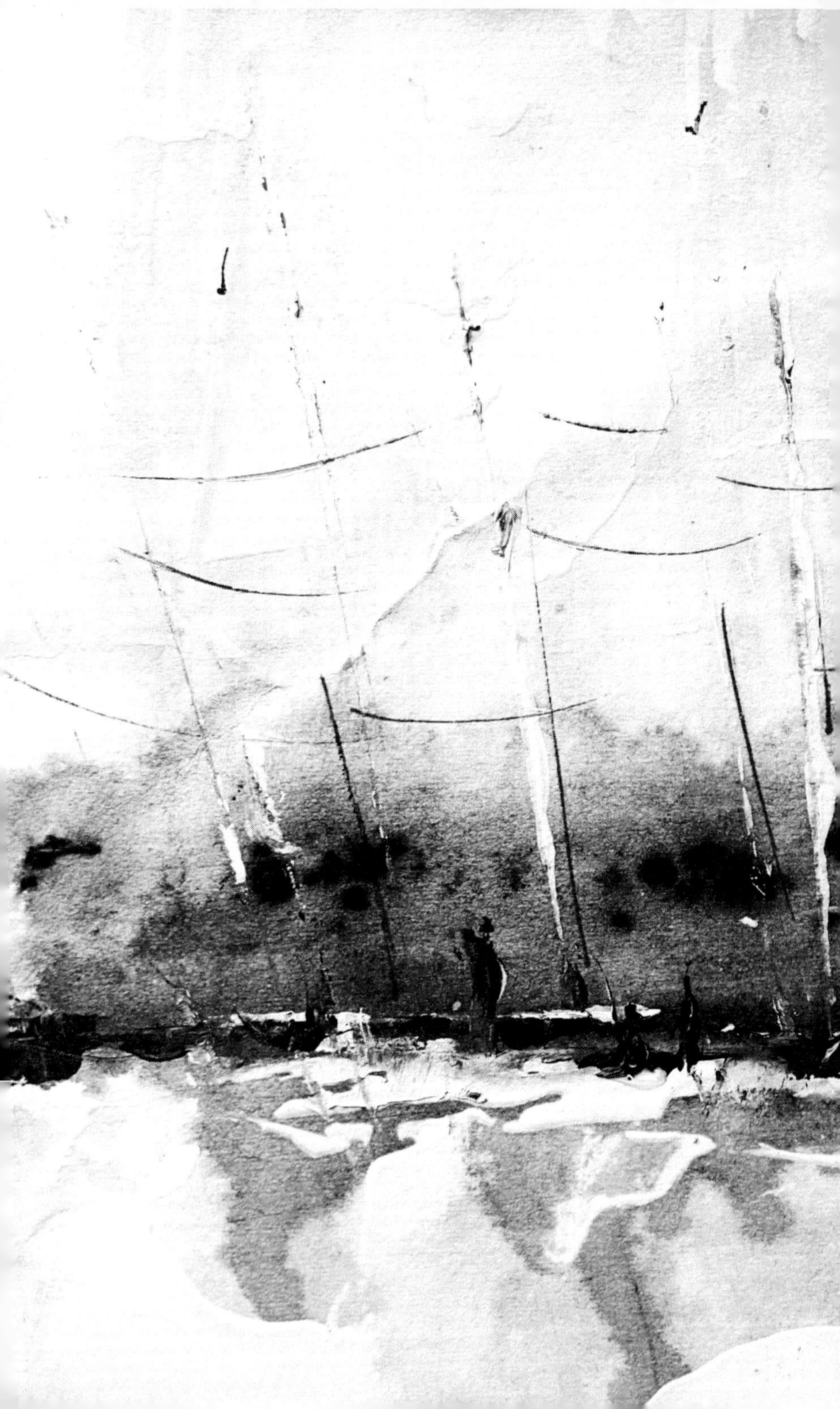

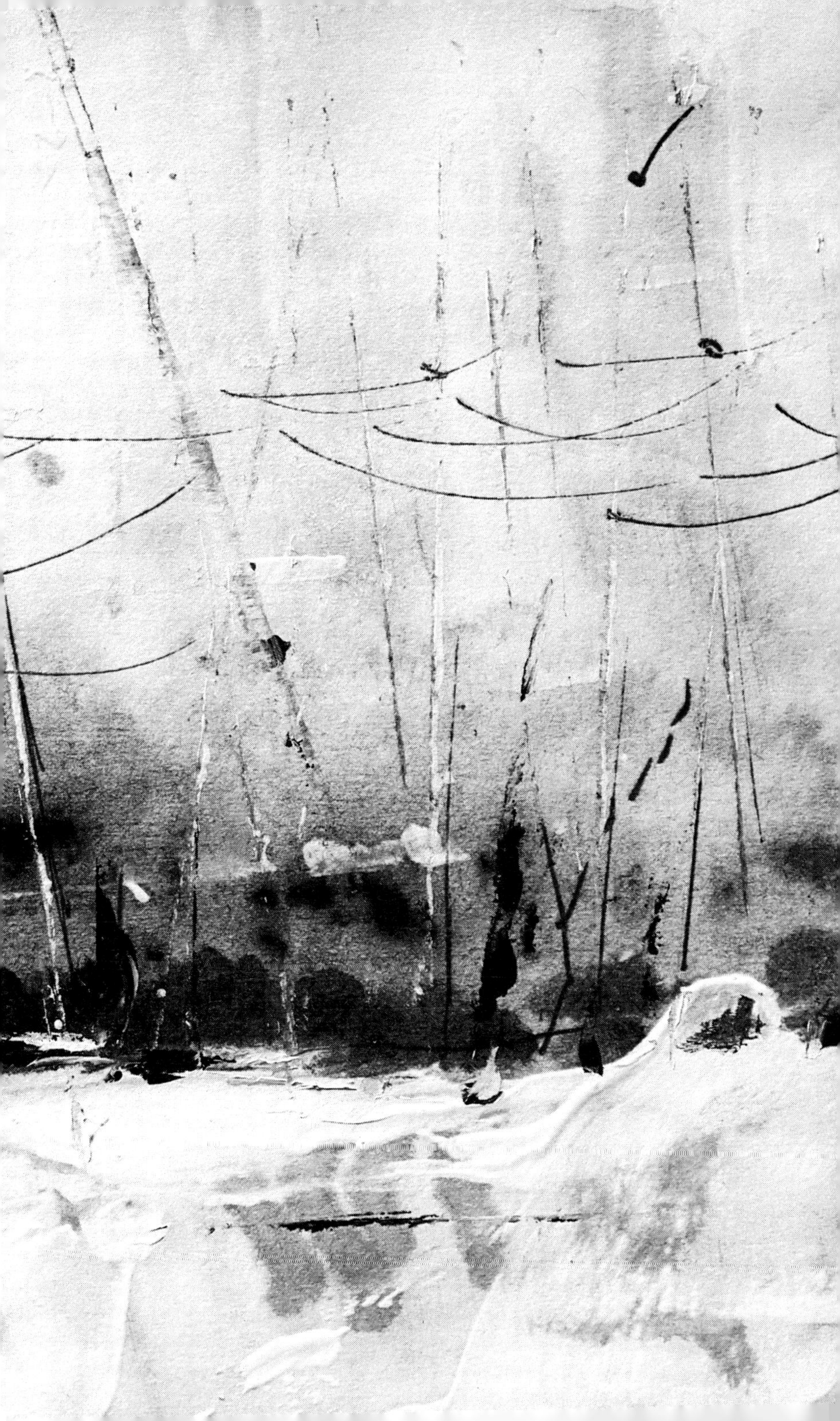

i have seen
another version of me
don’t worry dear,
i will handle you with care.

i am unconditional.
i am unfathomable.
i am vulnerable and real.
none of my part is dead.
i am love.

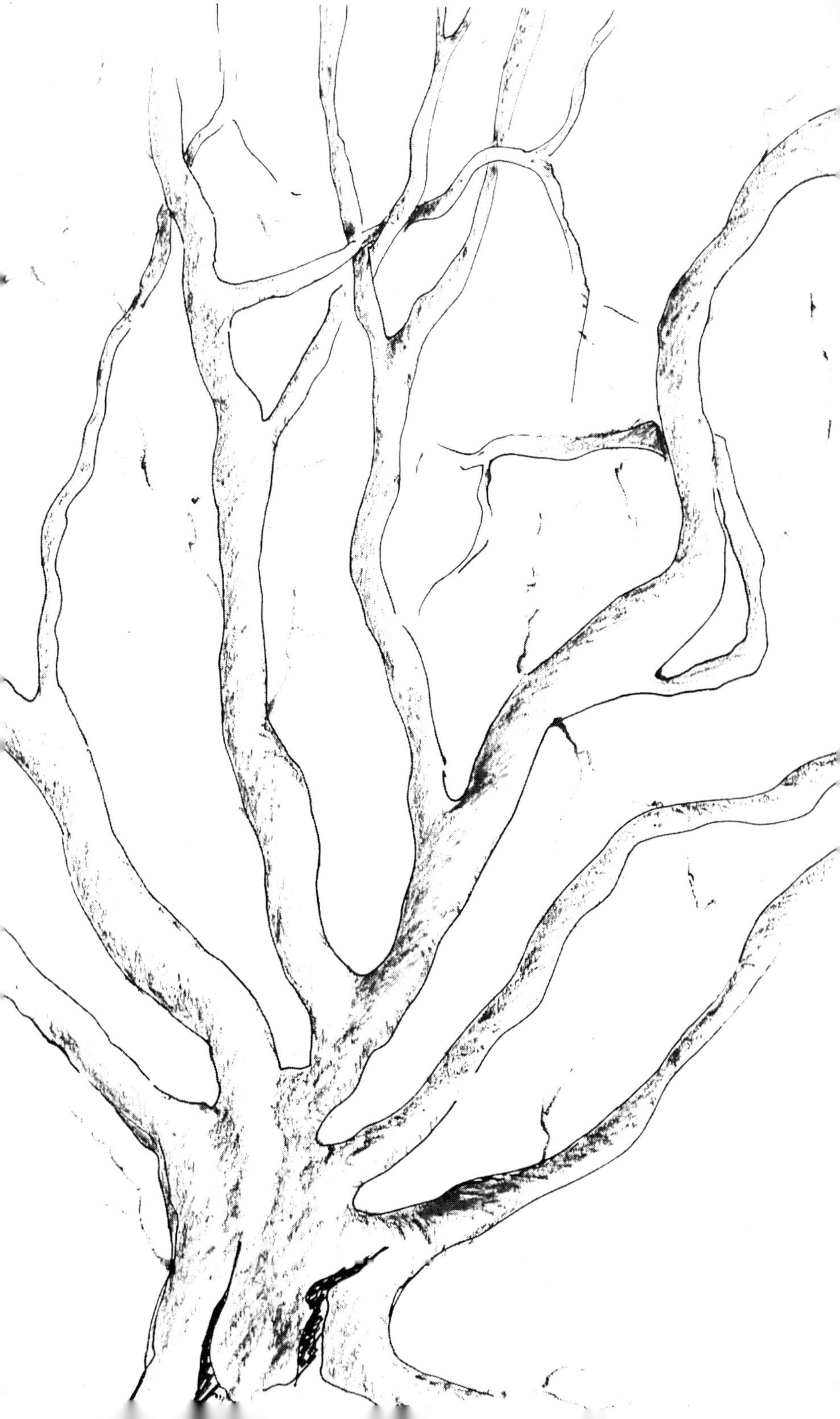

in my whole existence
they rectify my gestures
do's and don'ts create resistance
and my skin is never ready to apply
i am the body of harsh and unsteady textures
my eyes belong to the sky.

why overestimate the power of external love
when your body fulfils all your needs.

when i dance like a ballet dancer,
my smile enhances my weirdness,
for i am in love.

when you were unanswered for the reason of dejection.
you woke me up and i danced the whole nightwith felicity.

these days i sleep just to see you
and morning vibes makes it more meaningful.

creating my artworks is like
consuming painstaking pills
for boosting my immunity.

getting you was easier
than letting you go.
i decided to lose you
to get me back.

and sometimes you
have to move forth
beyond the society
to find your worth.

with you
i always felt lonely;

breathless and choked.

yes, i have changed
and this change is for finding happiness.

listen to the contentment
growing inside you,
other emotions are louder
and suppress the real ones.

what if i die
a hundred times
in each second
just to behold you?

i wonder
if i am still in love
or if i despise you the most
as you are never
not on my mind

the more i know you
the less it lets me sleep.

your melodious voice uplifts me
as you play romantic songs
pulling guitar strings,
strings of you and me.

heavy soul fake mask;
not allowing me to get a spark.

addiction and love are one word.
i am wild.

the seashore is calm,
the surge is quite,
your voice is a soothing melody to my insanity.

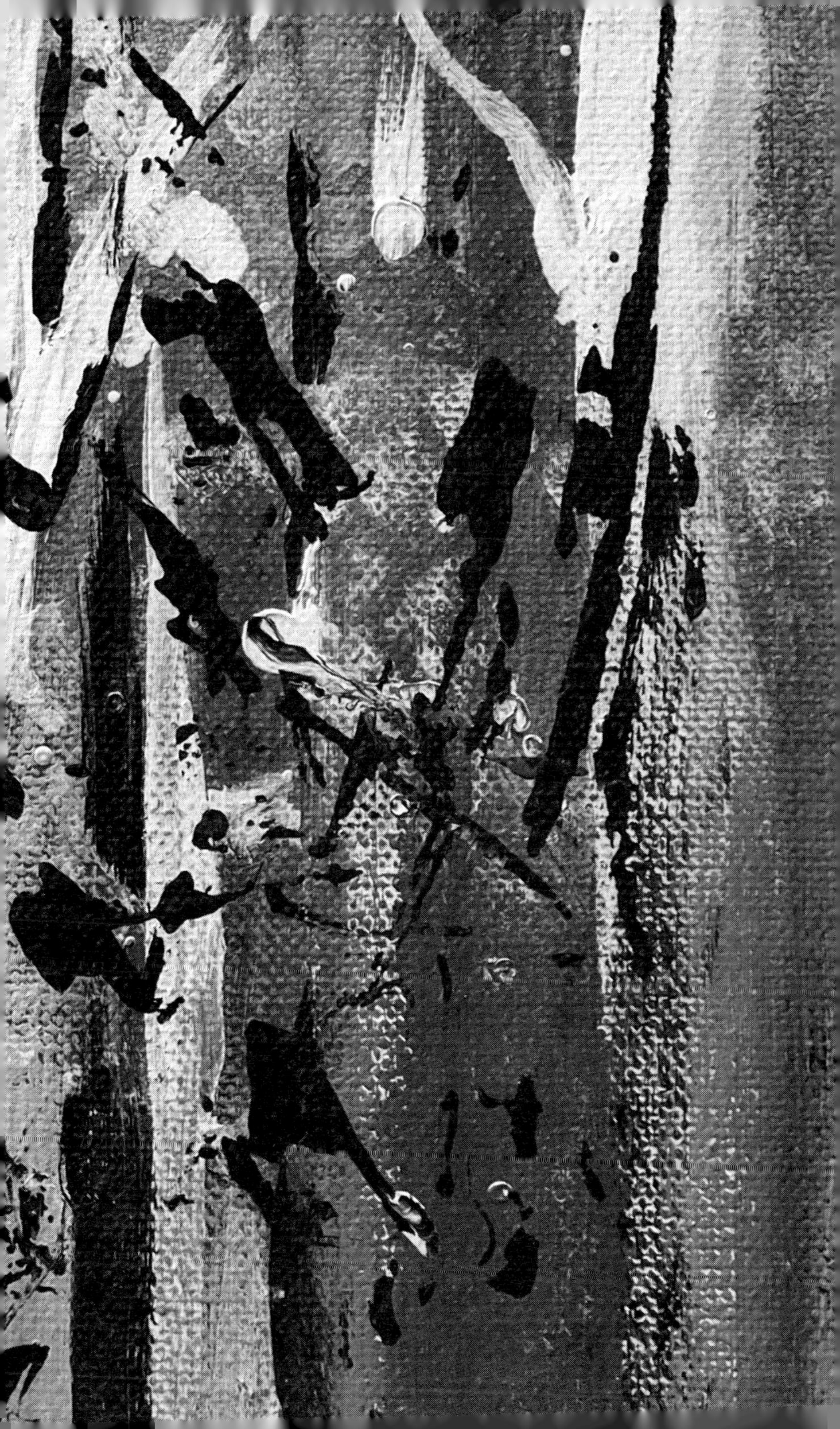

when you are fearful
and feel someone is pulling you from inside,
you are melting and yet have held the grip,
when you see nothing but pitch darkness,
and still stand upfront,
you are a winner not for others
but for yourself.

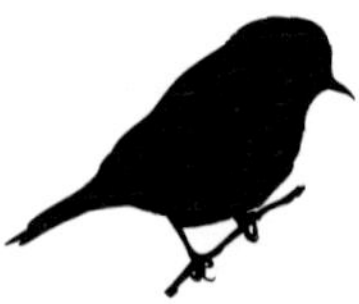

my entire body
is lighting with a blaze,
the fire of my dreams
which i see with open eyes.

artline gives the detail
to my creatives,
similarly, you enhance me
in your poems.

my skin breathes in the open air
and nurturing flowers grow on me.

sailing in a boat
in the misty dawn,
feel the cold breeze on my
skin and sun-kissed rays;
i feel an aura inside.

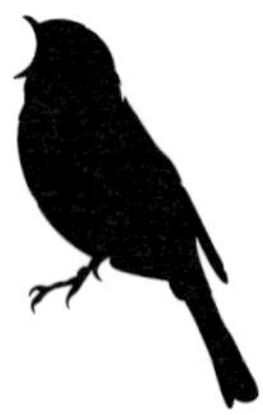

I have been in the body of mine
for so many years,
realized that
this is who stands by my side
and makes me stronger
even when i get bruises on my soul.

i regret not listening to myself,
and losing my worth
you always knocked me down
and now, i stand again.
i am the spectator of my success.

i remember the day
when i said i loved you,
with all my best efforts
and it drained me whole.

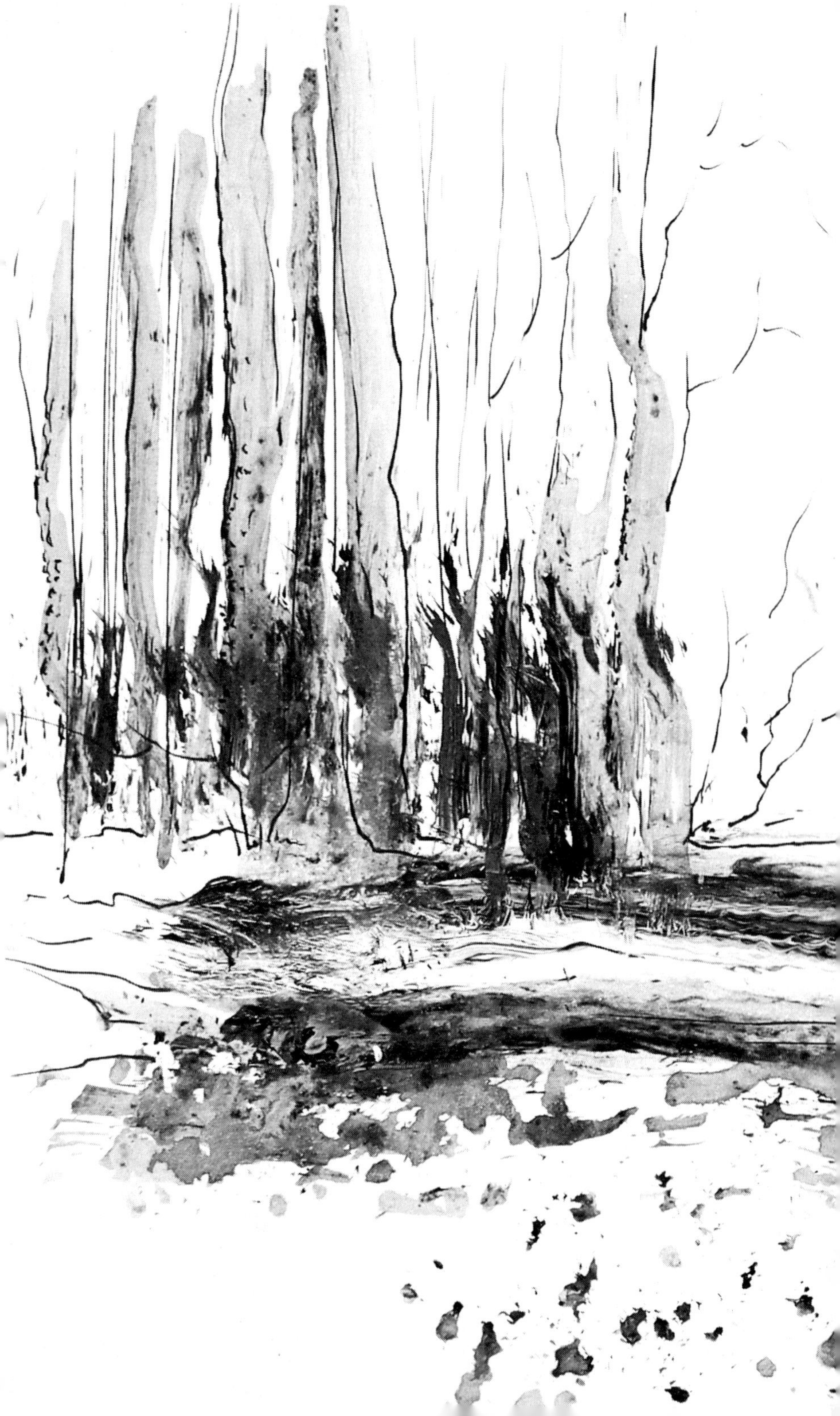

silence is so painful
it witnesses everything,
best and worst moments
and never lets out a word.

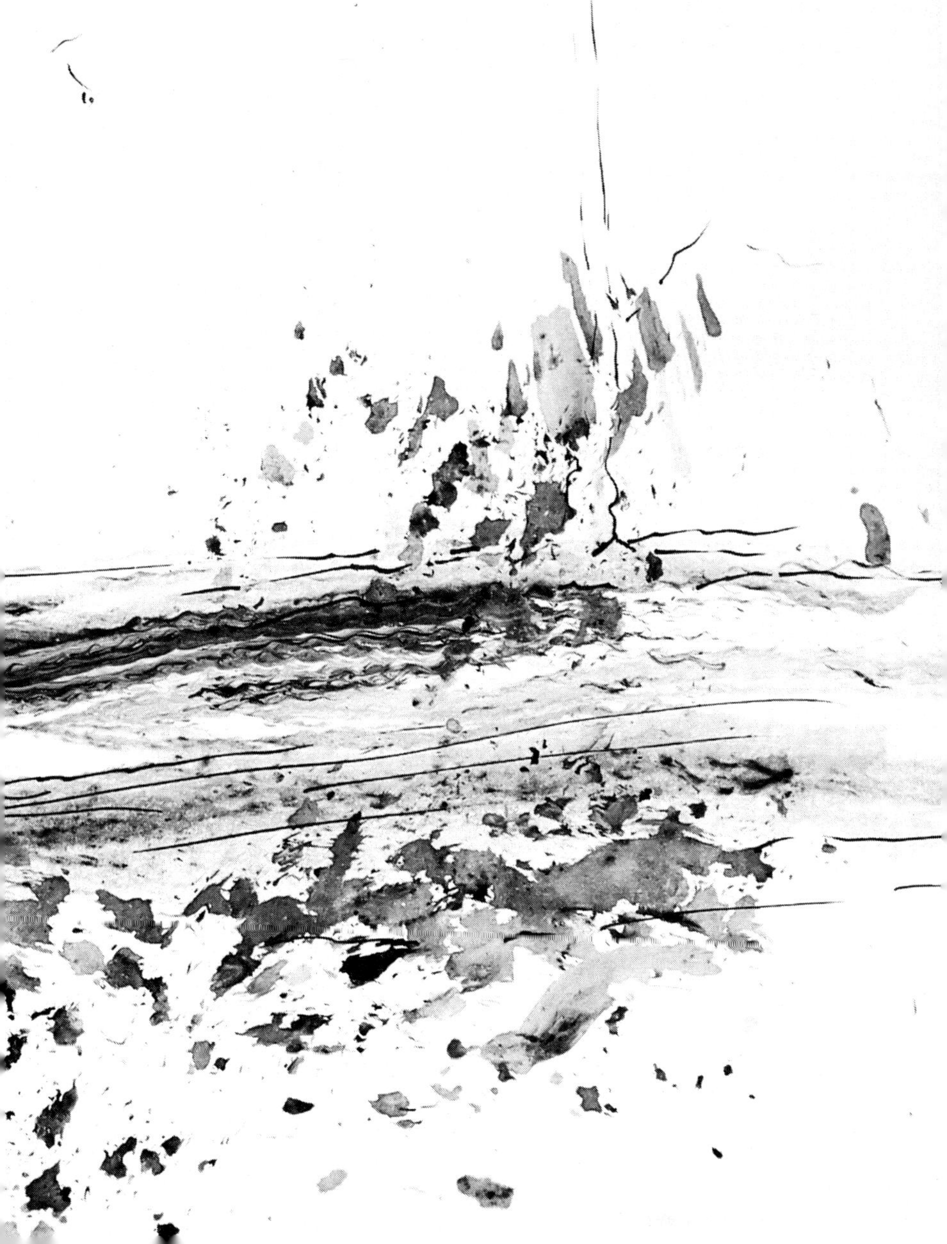

a part of me is still empty
the one you stole
my essence my entity.

loving you more than you deserved
was my weakness.

not loving you,
my signature.

you are the beauty and the beast,
you set the limits or set yourself free
from the thoughts that come and go.

searching you in every bit
you made me feel unwanted.

the more you fall,
the prettier you find your soul.
everything is within you.

love is the only emotion i inherited;
hatred was seeded by the species.

and then you realised
that whatever i did for you
was more than what you deserved.

i have not seen
the belief in your eyes for me
that made me a departed soul.

i stood so still
as a peaceful lake
you gave me ripples of joy,
the serene dusk of the day.

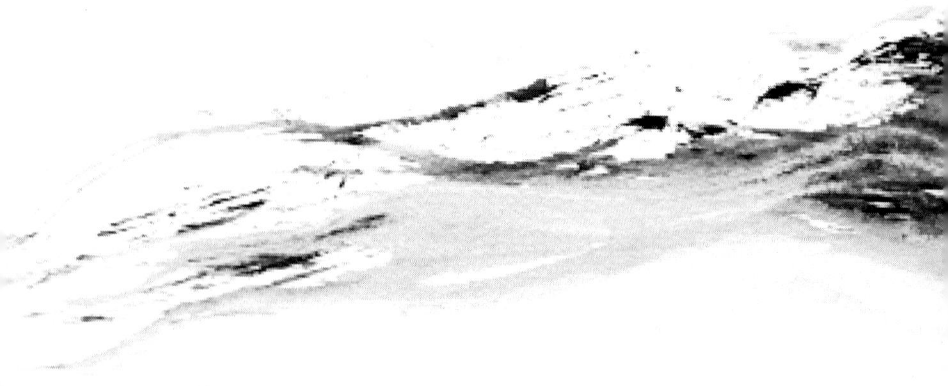

i was standing in the middle of a world
where only one color resides
red- the colour of blood.
where a heartless society believes
in destroying the entirety of humanity.
the horrible situation of my adorable land.

it is the love for myself
that guided me
to dig deep within
and recognize my calibre.

i may be cozy and comfortable,
you say you feel restful in my arms;
let go off all your worries,
and let the contentment make you calm.

i wish you craved me as you crave the canvas.
i wish...

remember:
what belongs to you will stay.

can you see the shimmer in my eyes?
i find you, when i see myself.

my soul and i are two parts of
me i believed you,
but my soul never allowed me to.

gone are the days
when i used to blush and sigh
just by your glimpse,
and found all the happiness
just by beholding you.

sitting by the river
during dawn and dusk
makes me calm.
feet dipped in
hands play with mist,
the sun rays tickles my skin,
i close my eyes,
allow you to come and pour within.

the love between us
had a very short life.
i wish i could water it
and collect some more moments.

i have moved so far
in process of finding oneself.
everyone touches the skin
none the soul,
and i screech,
'come back home.'

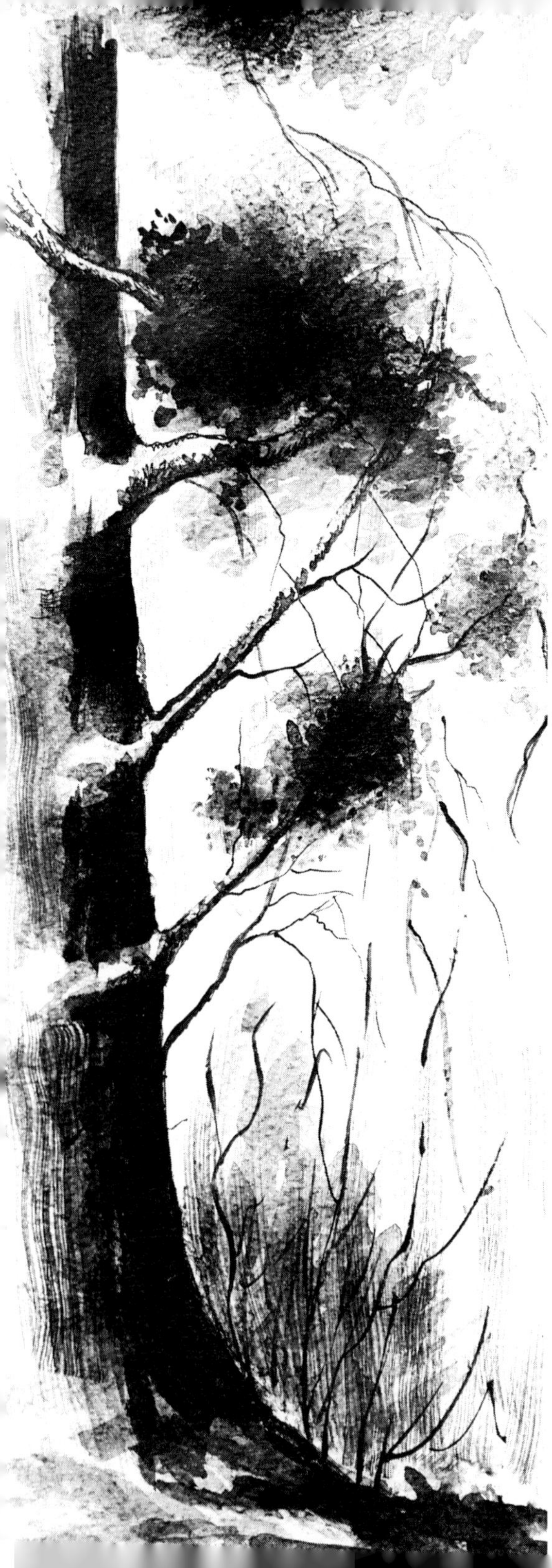

alas! you were
the temporary happiness
that gave a permanent mark of despair.

i harked back to all bonds
and grasped that you were not
a mere lovely part of it,
rather, you were my life.

winters are like a bride
beauty wrapped with grace,
snow, are the frills of the
gown gathered joy of entity.

my heart is empty now
i cared for you so much
the feeling is subsiding sobbing
feared and teared,
incapable of healing anymore.

you were my sky,
my whole cosmos.
you were and you are
precious to me.
you will always be.

every part of my body
bloomed like flowers
since the day you left
from my life.

you and i,
we are never together.
yet your impression
still holds my breath.

why am i not able to let you go?
to think, there is something left behind.
something incomplete maybe...

you make all my sorrows vanish
and give me relief
by residing in every part of my skin.

one sided love is a toxic mess.

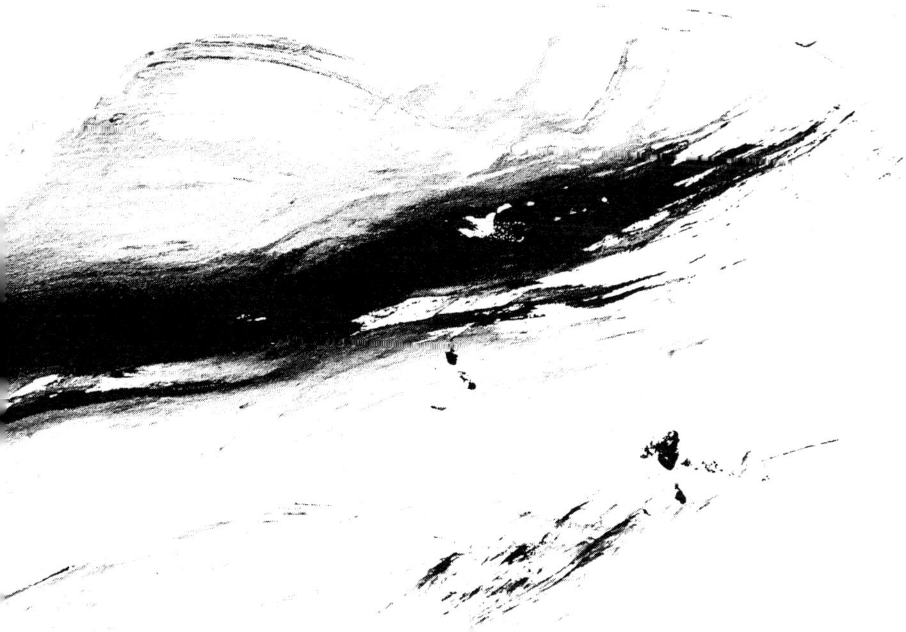

what if some pieces of me are left with you ?
you may have scrapped them off

but i still hold the shards
that you left impaled in me

love is where you can breathe

second wind

you are always there between my breaths

i remember you like a kiss on my
face, your essence in my sanity
which no one can replace

"what will you give me?"
he inquired.

if he insists himself to love me
it took me some time to understand
but i get that
it was not love.

you are playing the lead role
in your stage play
enact it well.

love is a meditation,

it's about connecting to the
soul, not the body.

while looking at the mirror
and praising the charm,
how could i forget
to admire the strength
that holds me firmly.

the harmony between you and i
is a free verse poetry

unrhythmic though heavenly

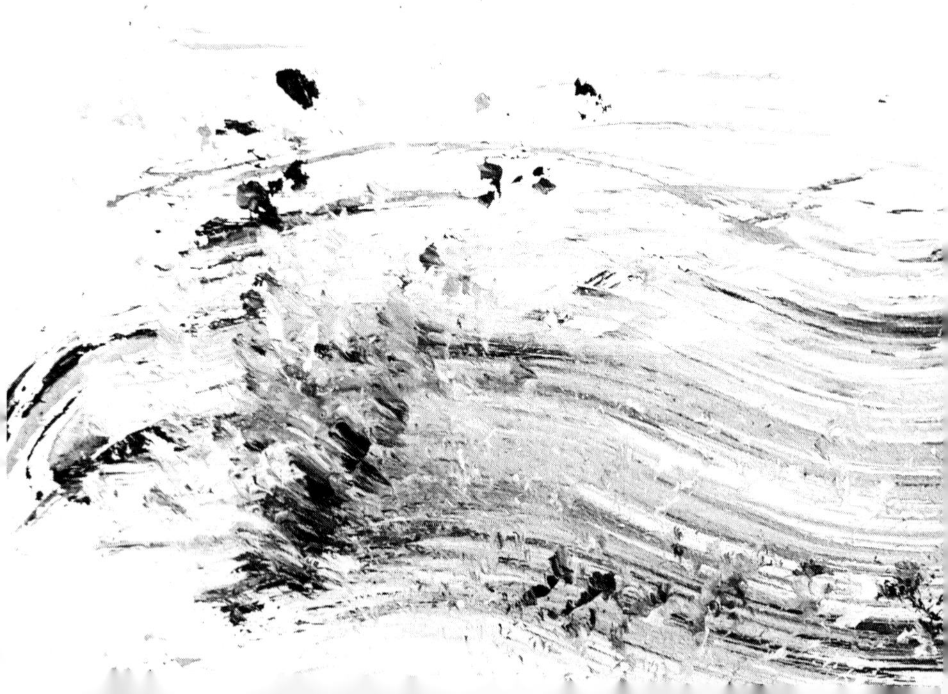

textures of the woods,
like fine wrinkles on my face
holds years of experience
with beautiful colours of all the seasons,
the buds, the flowers, i remember
what bloomed in me.

today, i am rootless, but still in love.

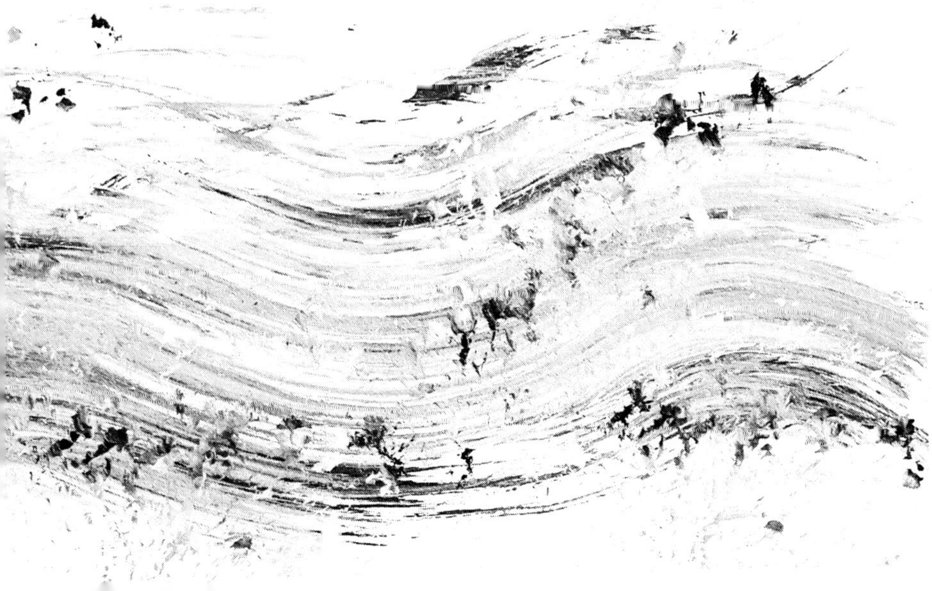

you are the cosmic soul on the earth,
you are not fragile.
so what if you are thin-skinned?
i pen down verses when i hold you.

you are never alone.
when you are sitting in a room
and you sense that my voice
whispers in your ears.
the aroma of me
takes you back to the days
when we were together.

rarest and fairest sweet pinkish-white
rose the day when you picked me
and put me in a vase
petals started tumbling
and you never glanced.
alas! your insensibility destroyed me.

when i loved you,
and you laughed,
you woke me up.
when i grieved,
and you chuckled,
you woke me up.
when i held your hand,
and you touched my body,
you woke me up.
when i talked,
and you never listened,
you woke me up.
you gave all the reasons to say,
'you woke me up.'

and i was searching
for your mist,
here and there.
sometimes flowers,
sometimes mud,
sometimes cushion,
sometimes bed.
i wonder why i was looking outside
when you are in my skin, always.

your body is a bliss
you have your shining wings
you fly free in the sky,
zypher kissed you, and you smile
loosen your body, close your eyes,
fall in a deep shell, and find yourself,
a polished pearl.

the meaning of myself
it was always love,

who empowered me
and never let me fall
and i always stayed strong.

the world is dying
with a dreadful disease,
and we are busy playing
the blame game.

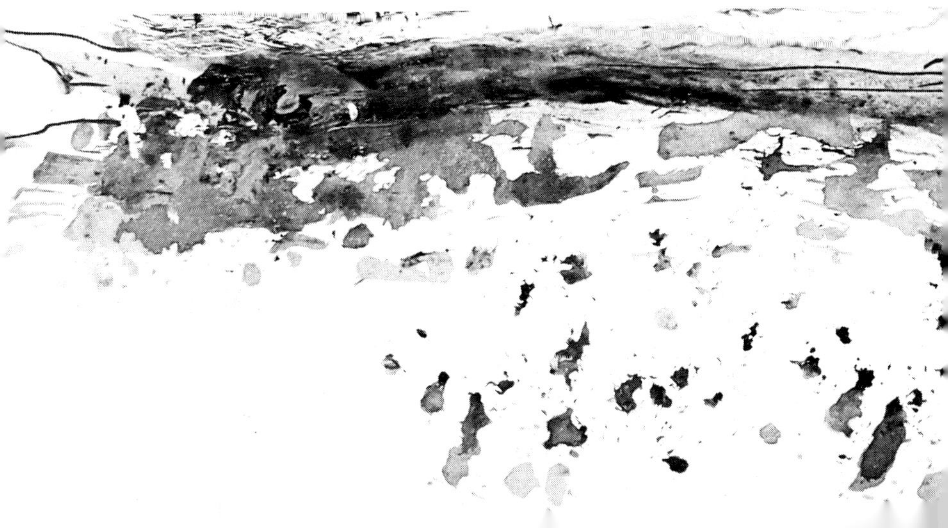

the blue window
where i stand and see up in the sky,
where birds fly, rainbow reside, sun shines,
twinkling stars and shimmering moonlight
where my dreams rest with the shiny cotton balls

i am the sky where you want to fly
i am your blue window;
the place of aspirations,
a veracity, which you never deny.

let's walk on the unknown path,
let's just not say a single word,
let's not discuss what makes us
apart, let's leave everything behind,
let's just feel the peace within,

let the serenity take over.

you are the magician.
look at the way you created yourself.

you begged to see
my true self
i peeled off my wounds
and in return
you turned your back at me
and left me to bleed.

full of orchids
rooted in my essence
elegantly planted
hope you find comfort
in the valleys of my body.

when you held me tight
on the last christmas night
and bent me in your arms;
my red attire moved like a charm
and when you kissed with love,
i was convinced that this will
be my favourite work of art.

i want to
see you
feel you
touch you
and hold you

so i write.

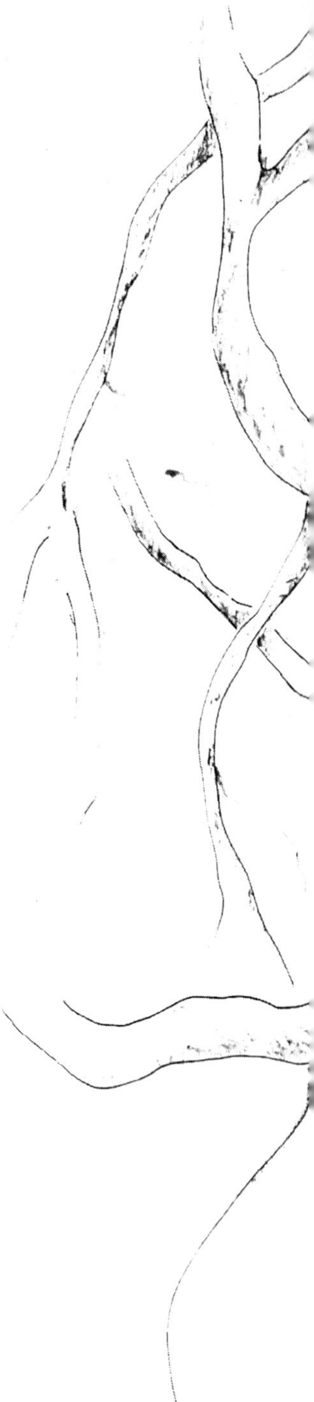

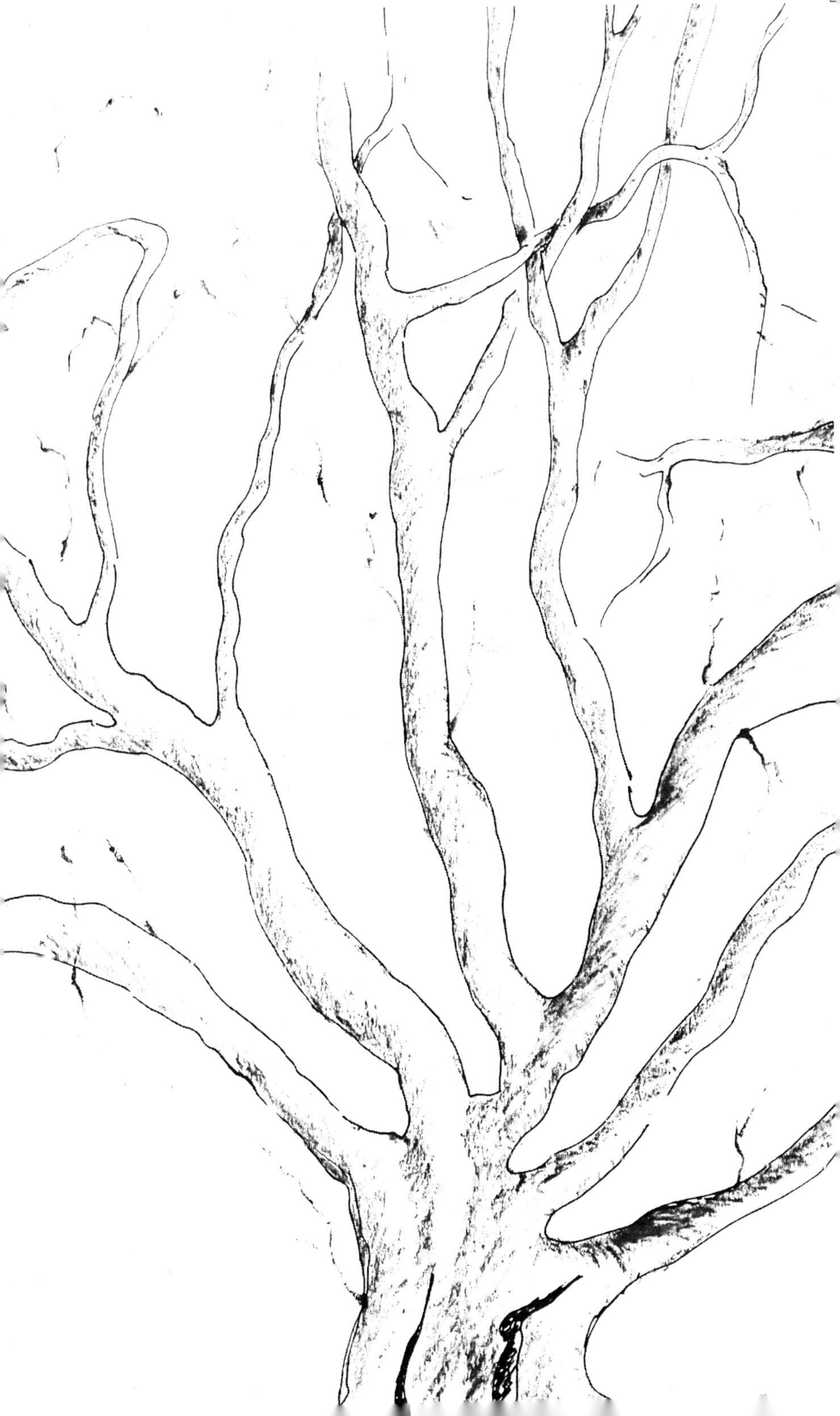

Acknowledgement

No matter how many times you have published a book, it will always be a different ride with each book. Although, the process of writing,

'Second Wind' was filled with many ups and downs, but I must say I was surrounded by best bunch of people who made it as easy as ABC.

I owe an enormous gratitude to my parents, my husband and my children who were and are always there to support me, inspire me, and provide me with necessary inputs on N-number of drafts

I'll forever be grateful to my mentor, guide, friend, and a great artist, Mrs. Jaskanwal Jit Kaur. Thank you for being a great assistance in whatsoever I do.

I'll forever indebt to my readers who appreciate my writings, provide me honest feedback and love me and my book from the core of their heart. I am nothing without you all, Love you.

Last but not the least, my publishers, who have given me valuable advice and guidance throught my publishing journey.

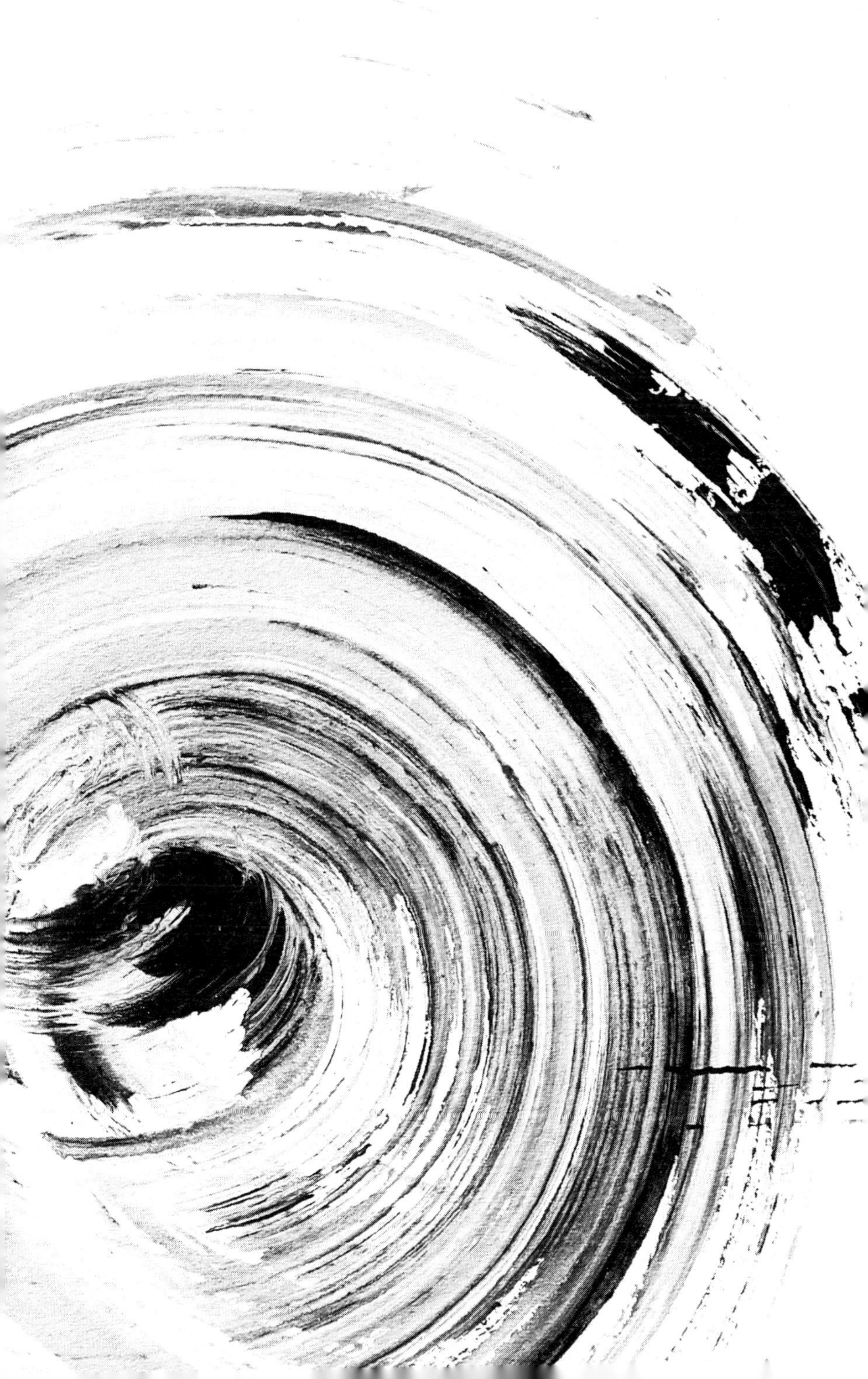

" 'Dear Self' is amazing, the poetess has written it so nicely in a very simple language even children can enjoy reading, with in depth meanings. Talks about reality some hard ones too, very motivating.
Its divided in 6 parts... I read 'Medley' and 'I am love' you feel like reading more and more....and more.....
Congratulations Preeti Bhargava for the great effort"

"A very thoughtful book with great poems.. Pleased to read the book...
Great work author Preeti Bhargava"

"Beautiful poems that's touch your heart.. I always read "Dear Self" when i am alone..
Thank you Preeti ji.."

"Thanks for changing the way we see the world with these amazing words. I would highly recommend this book to all."

"Loved the book .... It's something that u can relate to...the poems are lovely simple and yet has a deep meaning to. It ...a must buy"

"Very simply the best book one can add to ones collection"

“Amazing collection of poems which talks about self love. Felt so happy after reading each poem and finished the book in one go. Recommend this book to all”

“My son bought a signed copy of the book.... He loved it so much that he read it at one go... When a book is able to captivate an 11 year old that says a lot...
Simple language yet thought provoking...
Keep it up Preeti Bhargava.”

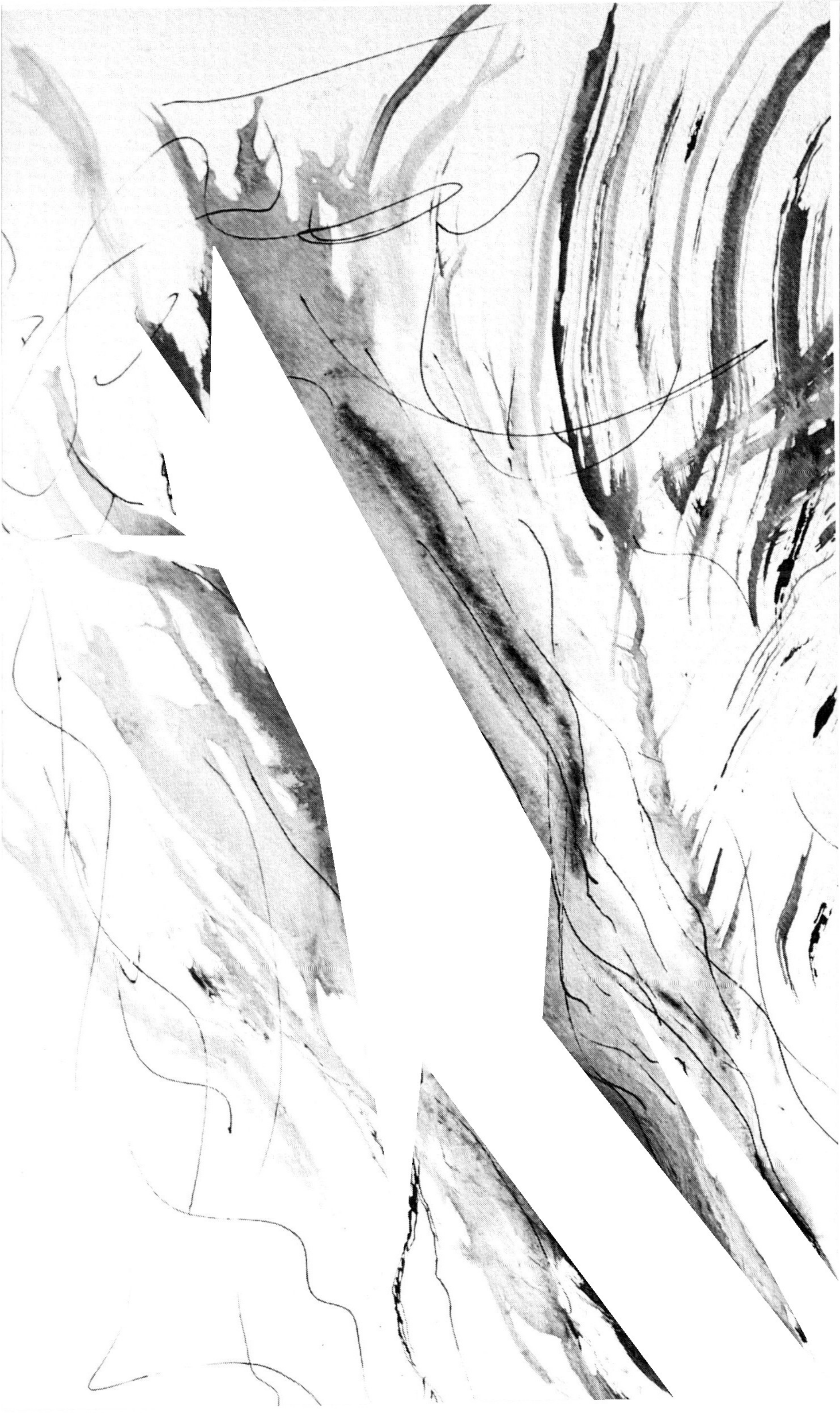

[let me rest at you by your side]